Lungs

Injury, Illness and Health

Carol Ballard

Heinemann
LIBRARY

www.heinemann.co.uk/library
Visit our website to find out more information about **Heinemann Library** books.

To order:
 Phone 44 (0) 1865 888066
 Send a fax to 44 (0) 1865 314091
 Visit the Heinemann Bookshop at www.heinemann.co.uk/library to browse our catalogue and order online.

First published in Great Britain by Heinemann Library, Halley Court, Jordan Hill, Oxford OX2 8EJ, part of Harcourt Education.

Heinemann is a registered trademark of Harcourt Education Ltd.

© Harcourt Education Ltd 2003
The moral right of the proprietor has been asserted.

Editorial: Nick Hunter and Catherine Clarke
Design: Jo Hinton-Malivoire and
Tinstar Design Limited (www.tinstar.co.uk)
Illustrations: Jeff Edwards except for p. 5 by Ken Vail Graphic Design
Picture Research: Maria Joannou and Su Alexander
Production: Viv Hichens

Originated by Ambassador Litho Ltd
Printed and bound in Hong Kong, China by South China Printing Company

ISBN 0 431 15716 2
07 06 05 04 03
10 9 8 7 6 5 4 3 2 1

British Library Cataloguing in Publication Data
Ballard, Carol
Lungs. – (Body Focus)
612.2
A full catalogue record for this book is available from the British Library.

Acknowledgements
The publishers would like to thank the following for permission to reproduce photographs:

Corbis pp. **38** (Dat's Jazz), **40** (Roger Ressmeyer); Corbis Royalty Free p. **15**; Corbis Stockmarket p. **7**; Getty Images p. **18** (Eyewire); Science Photo Library pp. **4**, **9**, **13** (David M Martin, M.D.), **14** (Matt Meadows/Peter Arnold), **17** (CNRI), **21** (Professor P Motts/G. Macchiarelli University 'Las Sapienza' Rome), **22** (top) (Gusto), **22** (bottom) (John Greim), **23**, **24** (Dr Kari Lounatmaa), **25** (Simon Fraser), **27** (Professor S Cinti/CNRI), **29** (CNRI), **31** (SBIP/Laurent/B. Hop Ame), **32** (Cape Grim B.A.P.S/Simon Fraser), **33** (Perlstein/Jerrican), **34** (left) (Astrid & Hanns-Frieder Michler), **34** (right) (Manfred Kage), **35** (Custom Medical Stock Photo) **43** (Geoff Tompkinson); Reuters p. **11** (Steve Marcus); Wellcome Trust p. **16**.

Cover photograph of a coloured X-ray of the lungs of a healthy person reproduced with permission of Science Photo Library.

The publishers would like to thank David Wright for his assistance with the preparation of this book.

Every effort has been made to contact copyright holders of any material reproduced in this book. Any omissions will be rectified in subsequent printings if notice is given to the publishers.

CONTENTS

Words appearing in the text in bold, **like this**, are explained in the Glossary.

THE RESPIRATORY SYSTEM

We need a constant supply of oxygen to stay alive. The respiratory system allows us to obtain oxygen from the air, and to get rid of waste carbon dioxide. It also enables us to speak and make other noises, and to do things such as blow up balloons and play wind instruments. The lungs are the main organs involved in the processes of breathing in (**inhaling**) and breathing out (**exhaling**). The **diaphragm**, ribcage and chest muscles are also important in the mechanism of breathing.

Inhaling and exhaling

When we inhale, air enters the body via the nose or mouth and passes into the top of the throat (the pharynx). This leads to the windpipe (trachea), which branches into two tubes called bronchi (each tube is called a **bronchus**) that lead into the lungs. In the lungs, the blood collects oxygen and releases carbon dioxide. When we exhale, air leaves the body via this route, in reverse. As air passes through the voice box (larynx) the vocal cords move and these movements make sounds. We control the volume and pitch of the sounds to talk, shout and sing.

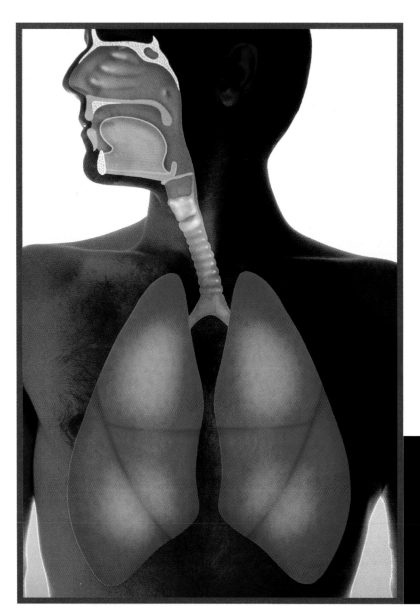

This artwork of the lungs and respiratory system, superimposed on to a photograph of a man's torso, shows how air is breathed in through the nose and mouth and travels down the trachea into the two lungs.

The ribs form a bony cage around the lungs, protecting them from injury. The ribcage is flexible and, together with associated muscles, it helps the lungs to expand and contract as we breathe in and out. The diaphragm is a strong, domed sheet of muscle and **tendon**-like material that forms a complete wall between the bottom of the chest and the top of the abdomen. It plays an important role in the breathing mechanism.

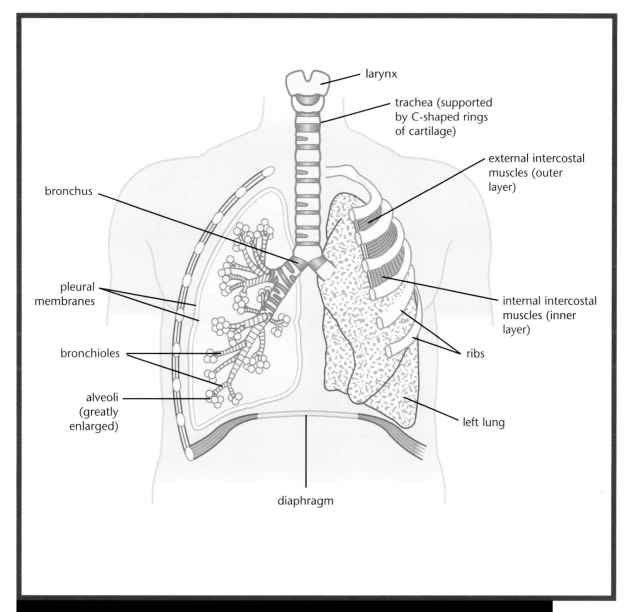

This picture shows the structures that make up the respiratory system. It also shows the ribcage and diaphragm – these are not part of the respiratory system, but they are essential in making the chest movements that enable us to breathe.

With the exception of some **micro-organisms**, every living thing needs oxygen in order to survive. It plays a key role in **aerobic respiration** (also called cellular respiration), a process that releases stored energy.

When we eat, our food is broken down into smaller and smaller pieces, until eventually it is separated into individual **molecules** that our bodies can use. These molecules are absorbed into the bloodstream, and transported to every part of the body. One of these molecules is glucose, a **carbohydrate**. Foods that contain a lot of glucose include biscuits, cakes, pasta, bread and rice. Other foods contain molecules that can be converted into glucose.

Aerobic respiration

When glucose reaches individual cells, the process of aerobic respiration can take place. This is a complicated chain of chemical changes, each step of which has its own special enzyme to help it to happen. An enzyme is a **protein** that speeds up a **chemical reaction** but does not get used up itself. Enzymes split glucose molecules into even smaller molecules. Oxygen joins with some of the molecules to make water and carbon dioxide, and the energy stored in the glucose molecule is released.

This can be summarized as an equation:

$$\text{glucose} + \text{oxygen} \longrightarrow \text{water} + \text{carbon dioxide} + \text{energy}$$
$$(C_6H_{12}O_6 + 6O_2 \longrightarrow 6H_2O + 6CO_2 + \text{energy})$$

The water made during aerobic respiration is absorbed by the body tissues. Excess water is transported in the bloodstream to the kidneys, where it leaves the body as urine when we go to the toilet. The carbon dioxide made during aerobic respiration is transported by the blood to the lungs, where it leaves the body when we breathe out.

The process of aerobic respiration is **exothermic**, with some of the released energy appearing as heat that is used to maintain our correct body temperature. The rest of the released energy is used to make a chemical called adenosine triphosphate (ATP). This is stored in the cells and they can use the energy when they need it, to drive other chemical reactions. Some of these just happen inside the cells without our being aware of them, but they are essential for keeping our bodies functioning normally. We are aware of the results of others – such as those that make muscles contract and relax, allowing us to move.

The more vigorously we work, the more energy our muscles use – so the more oxygen they need and the faster we breathe.

Respiration and exercise

When we exercise vigorously, our muscles need more energy, so aerobic respiration has to be speeded up to release it. The harder we work, the more oxygen we need so the faster we have to breathe. If we exercise too vigorously our muscles cannot get enough oxygen. Muscles can release energy by another process – **anaerobic respiration** – which does not need oxygen. During this process glucose is broken down into lactic acid, and energy is released.

$$\text{glucose} \longrightarrow \text{lactic acid} + \text{energy}$$
$$(C_6H_{12}O_6 \longrightarrow 2C_3H_6O_3 + \text{energy})$$

However, less energy is released than in aerobic respiration. Lactic acid is poisonous and must be broken down quickly into carbon dioxide and water – and this change needs oxygen.

$$\text{lactic acid} + \text{oxygen} \longrightarrow \text{carbon dioxide} + \text{water}$$
$$(2C_3H_6O_3 + 6O_2 \longrightarrow 6CO_2 + 6H_2O)$$

If too much lactic acid builds up in the muscles, they ache and you may get cramp. The build up of lactic acid, which is later broken down, is said to create an 'oxygen debt'. This means that, after exercise involving anaerobic respiration, extra oxygen is needed to bring everything back to normal.

MOUTH AND NOSE

Air enters and leaves the body via the mouth and nose. As air passes through the **nasal cavity** it is cleaned, warmed and moistened. We smell chemicals in the air as it passes through our nose and stimulates **sensory** cells.

The part of our face that we call our nose is made of plates of **cartilage** attached to the nasal bone of the skull. Cartilage is strong, giving the nose its shape, but it is also flexible, allowing the nose to bend. A piece of cartilage forms a central wall, making the two nostrils.

Inside the nose

When air enters the nostrils it first passes through the vestibule, the space immediately inside each nostril. This is lined by skin with coarse hairs that act as a filter, trapping particles of dust and dirt. The nostrils open into a chamber called the nasal cavity, the space below the base of the skull bone and above the roof of the mouth. The nasal cavity is lined with a special **membrane** called the nasal mucosa. This produces **mucus** to keep all the surfaces moist. Dust particles and **micro-organisms** that get past the hairs in the vestibule get trapped in the sticky mucus. The nasal mucosa also contains many tiny blood **capillaries**; as the blood flows through these, it warms the air.

At the top of the nasal cavity are two small areas, each about the size of a thumb nail, called the olfactory centres. These contain millions of olfactory cells. Long hairs called **cilia** stick out from these cells into the mucus layer. When chemicals in the air waft past them, they respond. The olfactory cells send electrical signals via the olfactory nerves to the brain. The brain interprets the signals and we 'smell' the chemical.

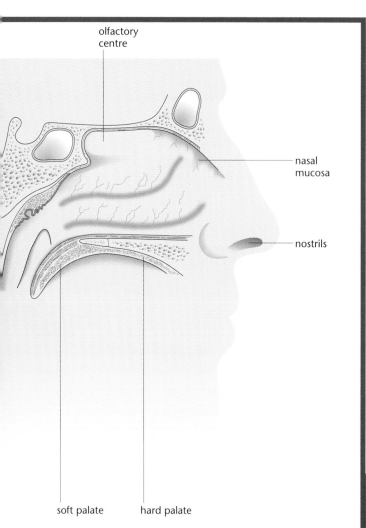

olfactory centre

nasal mucosa

nostrils

soft palate

hard palate

This picture shows the structures inside the mouth and nasal cavity.

Having a cold

When we have a bad cold, our sense of smell is often dulled. This is because the extra mucus in the nasal cavity prevents air circulating freely and stimulating the cilia. Sneezing and blowing the nose can help to remove excess mucus. Because the senses of taste and smell are closely linked, the flavours of our food often seem less strong when we have a cold.

Crying

The tear ducts from the eyes drain into the nasal cavity. Normally, the fluid drains away, but when we cry we produce too much fluid for this to happen. Some tears spill over and roll down our face, but some drain into the nasal cavity, overloading it. That is why you need to blow your nose when you have been crying.

Sinuses

The skull also has air spaces called **sinuses**. These are linked to the nasal cavity and are lined with mucus membranes. They are important when we talk or sing because they help make sounds fuller and richer.

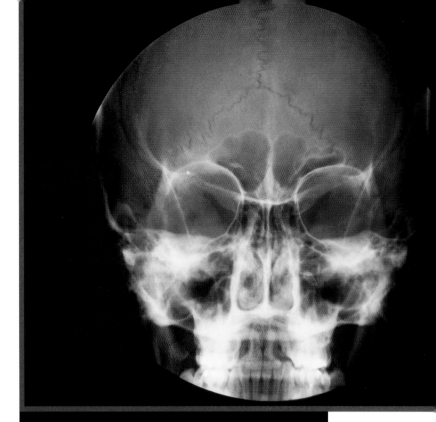

In this X-ray, the skull bones show up as solid white. The sinuses are the dark areas.

Decongestants and sport

If the membranes of the sinuses become inflamed because of an infection or **allergic reaction**, they swell. This can block the openings into the nasal cavity, and stop mucus draining away. As mucus builds up in the sinuses, we suffer a sinus headache. **Decongestant** drugs can be taken to help to clear the sinuses. Many of these can be bought without a doctor's prescription – but anybody taking part in sporting events should be very careful as some of them contain substances that are banned in competitions.

PHARYNX AND LARYNX

After passing through the **nasal cavity**, air moves into the pharynx, the area at the back of the mouth and the top of the throat. The larynx (voice box) is at the lower part of the pharynx.

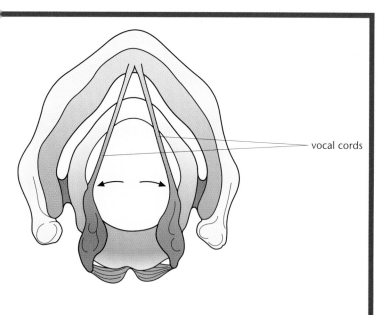

vocal cords

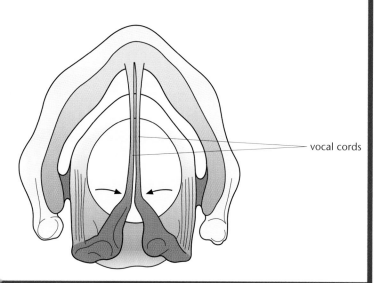

vocal cords

These diagrams show how the vocal cords work. In the top diagram, there is a space between the vocal cords so they do not vibrate as air rushes past them – no sound is made. In the bottom diagram, the vocal cords are touching and air passing them will make them vibrate – a sound is produced.

The pharynx is a funnel-shaped tube about 13 centimetres long. Its wall is made of muscle, arranged in an outer circular layer (rings of muscle) and an inner longitudinal layer (columns of muscle) and it is lined with a moist mucous **membrane**. The pharynx has three main parts:

• The upper part of the pharynx lies behind the soft palate. When food is swallowed, the flexible soft palate moves upwards to block off the entrance to the pharynx.

• The middle part of the pharynx carries air from the nasal cavity and mouth to the trachea (windpipe). It also carries food from the mouth to the foodpipe (oesophagus). When food is swallowed, a flap of elastic **cartilage** – the epiglottis – moves downwards to block off the entrance to the trachea. It moves upwards again to allow air to enter the trachea. The tonsils form a broken ring around the entrances to the oesophagus and trachea. They are involved in fighting infections, preventing foreign substances entering the body by destroying them.

• The lower part of the pharynx connects with the trachea. It is lined with a mucous membrane to keep it moist, and has **cilia** to trap dust and other particles.

Adam's apple

The larynx is at the bottom of the pharynx. The walls of the larynx are made of nine pieces of stiff, curved cartilage. The largest is the thyroid cartilage (Adam's apple), which can be seen beneath the skin at the front of the neck. It is larger in men than in women because male **hormones** stimulate its growth during puberty, but female hormones do not. These pieces of cartilage provide a framework for the vocal cords. Vocal cords are two thin strips of tough material that are stretched across the larynx from front to back.

Vocal cords

If we are just breathing normally, the vocal cords are apart so there is no noise. When we want to make a sound, muscles in the neck alter the position of the cartilage frame, stretching the vocal cords and moving them together to narrow the gap between them. As air rushes past them, they vibrate, making a noise. Because of the angle of the vocal cords as we **exhale**, it is easier to produce a sound when we are breathing out than when we are breathing in. The tighter the vocal cords are stretched, the faster they vibrate and the higher the sound produced. Because women's vocal cords are usually shorter and thinner than men's, their voices are higher.

On stage, singers must have great control over the larynx, to allow production of exactly the right sounds.

TRACHEA AND BRONCHI

After passing through the larynx, air moves into the trachea. This branches into two narrower tubes, the primary bronchi. These branch again to form the secondary bronchi and more and more branching eventually ends with the narrowest tubes, the **bronchioles**.

The trachea is a tube, about 12–13 centimetres long, and 2–3 centimetres in diameter. It is surrounded by a column of C-shaped rings of **cartilage** that give it support and prevent it collapsing. The rings are connected by stretchy fibres and muscles, so the trachea is flexible and can bend and stretch as we move. The inside of the trachea is lined with mucous **membrane**, which produces **mucus** to keep the trachea lubricated and moist. It also has **cilia** that help to trap and remove any dust particles or **micro-organisms** that enter it.

The trachea branches into the right primary **bronchus**, leading into the right lung, and the left primary bronchus, leading into the left lung. These primary bronchi are also supported by rings of cartilage and are lubricated by mucus.

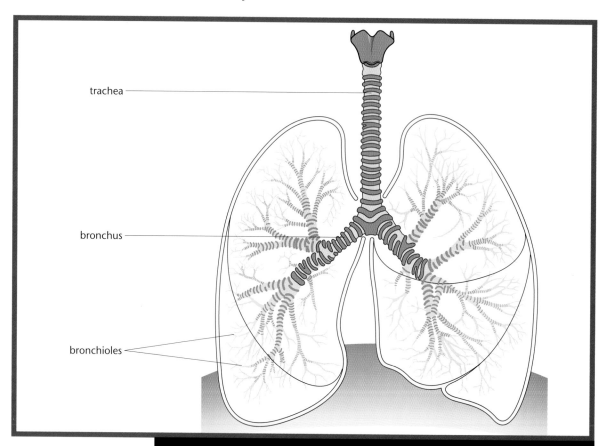

trachea

bronchus

bronchioles

In this picture, you can see how the trachea branches into two bronchi, and they in turn branch into the bronchioles.

At the point where the trachea branches is a small ridge called the carina. The mucous membrane here is very sensitive and is the most likely area of the trachea to trigger a cough when stimulated by foreign material, such as dust.

Into the lungs

Inside the lungs, the primary bronchi branch again to form smaller secondary bronchi. The lungs are divided into smaller areas called lobes. There is one secondary bronchus for each lobe of each lung – two for the left lung and three for the right. These branch again into even smaller tertiary bronchi, which then branch into bronchioles. As this branching continues, with the

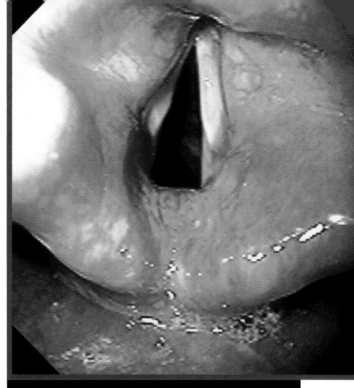

An endoscope allows doctors to see the lining of the airways. This picture shows the vocal cords in the larynx.

passages becoming narrower and narrower, the cartilage rings disappear and the amount of muscle in the walls of the tubes increases. Eventually, the branching ends with the narrowest tubes of all, the terminal bronchioles.

If you look at the trachea, bronchi and bronchioles upside down, the branching pattern looks rather like a tree – so these structures are often called 'the bronchial tree'.

Emergency!

The trachea may be blocked as the result of a chest injury, inflammation or a swallowed object. This needs emergency treatment to enable the patient to breathe.

If the blockage is above the larynx, doctors may carry out a tracheotomy. A small cut is made in the neck below the larynx, and a tube is inserted. The patient can then breathe, as air can enter and leave the lungs via this tube.

Alternatively, a tube can be inserted via the mouth or nose and pushed down through the larynx and trachea. The tube pushes obstructions out of the way and sucks out any excess mucus, allowing the patient to breathe normally again. This procedure is called intubation.

RESPIRATORY NOISES

A rush of air through the respiratory system can result in several different noises being made. Some of these we can control, but some are completely uncontrollable!

Sneezing forces air, mucus, dust and micro-organisms out of the nose at high speed.

Sneeze

A sneeze is a sudden involuntary exhalation of air through the nose, usually in response to excess **mucus** or dust particles in the **nasal cavity**. Air is forced out at a tremendous speed – up to 160 kilometres per hour – this is greater than the force of a hurricane!

When we sneeze, we **inhale**, and then the back of the tongue blocks the airway to trap the air. Abdominal muscles contract, increasing the pressure inside the chest space. This pressure then forces the air out through the nose. Mucus, dust and **micro-organisms** are carried out too and may travel several metres; using a handkerchief to trap our own droplets of mucus and germs from a sneeze prevents them spreading through the air for other people to breathe in.

Cough

Like a sneeze, a cough is a sudden involuntary exhalation of air – but via the mouth instead of the nose. We usually cough in an attempt to dislodge excess mucus, dust particles or other foreign objects from the airways.

When we cough, we inhale, and muscles in the pharynx and larynx contract to trap the air. Pressure inside the chest increases as the abdominal muscles contract. The pharynx and larynx muscles relax, the airways open and air is forced out. As it passes through the larynx, the vocal cords vibrate and make a noise. Mucus is ejected from the airways and is usually swallowed or removed by spitting (again, using a handkerchief to catch our own germs is hygienic).

Hiccup

Nearly everybody will have experienced hiccups at some time and know just how uncontrollable they are! Hiccups are the result of sudden short contractions of the **diaphragm**. Air is sucked in so quickly that the epiglottis snaps shut noisily.

Sometimes, hiccups occur when the stomach is very full and irritates the diaphragm and nerves above it. Sometimes, they occur for no apparent reason.

An attack of hiccups is usually over in a few minutes; sometimes holding your breath for a short time can help to stop them by forcing the diaphragm to remain still.

Yawning is a way to quickly take oxygen into the lungs after exhaling, but it can also be a sign of boredom!

Snore

Snoring occurs when the throat muscles are relaxed, and the upper airway is partly blocked by the soft palate and the uvula (a flap of soft tissue that hangs down from the soft palate.) As the person breathes in and out, the soft palate and the uvula vibrate noisily as air passes over them.

Snoring is often worse when people sleep on their backs; turning on to the side, or changing the angle of the head can often reduce it. Nasal **decongestants** can sometimes help, and a variety of clips and pegs for the nose are available, which may also be of use for some people.

Yawn

There are several things that may cause us to yawn – but it is not clear whether one is more important than the others. We usually yawn when we are tired, bored or sitting in a stuffy room.

If we are sitting still and quietly, our breathing rate may slow down, so that carbon dioxide levels build up. Yawning rapidly clears any excess carbon dioxide out of the lungs.

If our breathing rate is slow, or the atmosphere is stuffy, we may not be taking in enough oxygen. Yawning rapidly fills the lungs with a fresh supply of oxygen.

When we yawn, many muscles of the face contract and then relax. This may stimulate the blood supply to the head, including the brain, and help us to feel more alert again.

The pharynx, larynx, trachea and bronchi can all be affected by infectious **bacteria** and **viruses**, and can be irritated by dust and smoke. Problems may develop quickly (acute) or slowly and last for months or years (chronic).

Pharyngitis

Pharyngitis is the medical term for a sore throat. Acute pharyngitis is usually the first sign of a viral infection such as the common cold or **influenza**. A bacterium, *streptococcus*, can also cause a sore throat usually known as 'strep throat'. Infections from other nearby sites, such as tonsils and **sinuses**, can also affect the pharynx. Chronic pharyngitis is usually caused by smoking and drinking too much alcohol.

Antibiotics can quickly clear up a bacterial infection, but have no effect on a viral infection or chronic pharyngitis. Comfort remedies, such as warm drinks and throat lozenges, can help to ease the soreness.

Laryngitis

Laryngitis means inflammation of the larynx. Acute laryngitis is usually caused by an infection, such as influenza or a common cold, or by violent shouting or singing. Irritation of the larynx by cigarette smoke can also lead to laryngitis. Chronic laryngitis is most commonly the result of irritation by tobacco smoke or dust, or by using the voice too much over a long period.

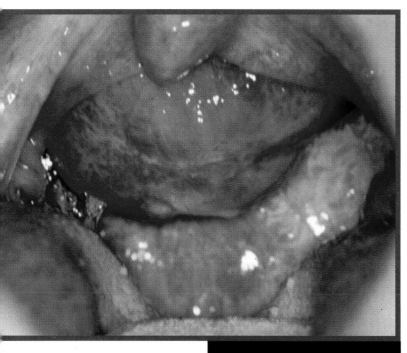

This photograph shows a polyp on the larynx.

Laryngitis is usually cured by resting the voice completely for a few days; inhaling warm steam can often help, too.

Polyps and nodes

Polyps are tiny, berry-like lumps that can develop on the vocal cords, making the voice sound hoarse and breathy. Vocal cord nodes are also tiny lumps, developing from over-use of the voice over a long period of time – raising the voice in a classroom for years means that many teachers suffer from these and so they are often called 'teacher's nodes'. Both polyps and nodes can be surgically removed.

Tonsillitis

Tonsillitis is an inflammation of the tonsils, usually caused by *streptococcus* bacteria, but sometimes caused by a virus. The tonsils swell and produce pus; the throat feels uncomfortable, making it hard to swallow. Some patients also suffer from earache and a stiff neck as the eustachian tube, which connects the ear and throat, may become blocked.

Tonsillitis is most common in young children and during puberty. This may be because the tonsils grow during childhood, but then begin to shrink at puberty. Pain can be relieved with warm drinks and antibiotics can cure bacterial infections. If a child suffers repeated infections, doctors may decide that the tonsils should be surgically removed.

Bronchitis

The main cause of chronic bronchitis is cigarette smoking. The smoke irritates the lining of the bronchi and they produce a lot of sticky **mucus**. This blocks the airways and prevents the **cilia** working normally; any **micro-organisms** that reach the bronchi are therefore not removed and are able to multiply and cause infection.

Bronchitis causes a persistent cough, often with wheezing and shortness of breath. Patients with bronchitis find it difficult to exercise or play sports and, in severe cases, just walking up stairs or moving around a room is difficult. Treatments include breathing exercises and oxygen therapy – where a patient's oxygen intake is increased by supplying pure oxygen via a face mask.

Emphysema

Patients with emphysema find any kind of exertion difficult as they are always breathless. Everyday activities can cause attacks of breathlessness, followed by coughing. The alveoli become permanently stretched and filled with air so the lungs become less elastic. Emphysema cannot be cured, but oxygen treatment can help and some drugs can clear the airways.

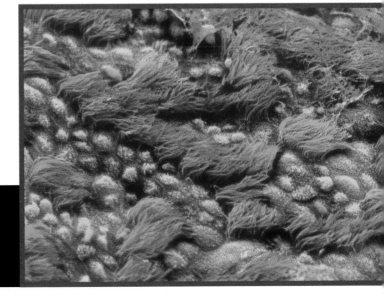

In this picture, taken using an endoscope, you can see the cilia that keep the airways clear of dust and micro-organisms.

LUNGS

The lungs are inside the chest, protected by the ribcage. They are pale-pink, spongy organs, each roughly cone-shaped with a narrow tip and a wide base. They are surrounded by **membranes** and fluid that lubricates them, allowing them to move freely during breathing.

Lung protection

The lungs are protected by a bony cage made by twelve pairs of ribs, by the **sternum** (breastbone) and the thoracic **vertebrae** (upper backbone). The first ten pairs of ribs are connected to the sternum by flexible strips of **cartilage**, allowing them to move. The bottom two pairs of ribs are 'floating ribs' and have no connection to the sternum. The ribs are moved as the muscles to which they are connected contract and relax, increasing and then decreasing the space inside the ribcage as we breathe in and out.

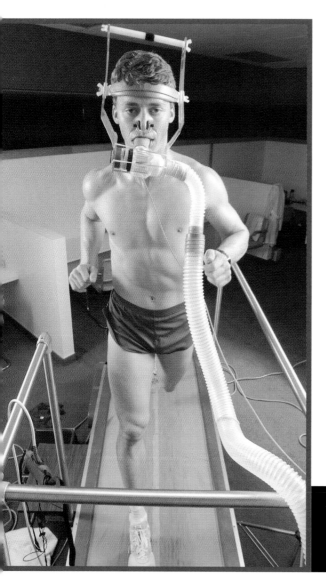

Inside the lungs

The lungs fill most of the space inside the chest. Each lung is enclosed and protected by a **pleural membrane**. These have two layers, with a space between them called the pleural cavity; this contains pleural fluid, a liquid produced by the membranes. Pleural fluid reduces friction between the membranes so they can slide easily over each other when we breathe. The pleural membranes may become inflamed, causing an illness called pleurisy.

The narrow tip of each lung is called the apex; the wide base of each lung is concave, to fit over the dome-shaped **diaphragm**. The right lung has three lobes – upper (superior), middle and lower (inferior). The left lung is slightly smaller than the right lung as it has a small hollow in which the heart lies; it has only two lobes – superior and inferior.

This athlete is using a spirometer to measure his lung capacity. It will record how much air he breathes in and out as he runs on the treadmill.

The left and right lung are joined in the centre by an area called the hilus, or root. Here, **bronchi**, major blood vessels, lymphatic vessels (allowing drainage of excess fluid) and nerves enter and exit each lung.

The amount of air the lungs can hold is called the **lung capacity**. It can be measured using a spirometer or respirometer, and recorded on a chart recorder or monitor. The trace that is shown is called a spirogram.

Lung capacity

The lungs of a healthy adult man can hold about 6 litres of air, but we cannot use all of this capacity. Several measurements can be made:

- when resting, an adult usually breathes in and out about 12–15 times every minute. With each breath, about 0.5 litres of air enters and leaves the lungs. This is the 'tidal volume'.
- there is always some air left in the lungs. This is the 'residual volume' and is usually about 1.2 litres.
- the maximum amount of air that can be breathed out after taking the deepest possible breath is about 3.5–4.5 litres and is called the 'vital capacity'
- the maximum amount of air that the lungs can hold is about 6 litres. This is the lung capacity.

In normal breathing, we only use a small fraction of our full lung capacity. When we exercise, we need to increase the amount of air that we breathe in and out. You can do this by breathing more quickly, or by breathing more deeply. When you breathe normally, about 0.15 litres of air gets no further than the nasal passages, trachea, bronchi and bronchioles and cannot be used by the body.

This table shows why slow, deep breathing is much more efficient than fast, shallow breathing.

	Fast and shallow 50 breaths / min	20 breaths / min	Slow and deep 10 breaths / min
Air in with each breath	0.2 litres	0.5 litres	1 litre
Total air in	50 x 0.2 = 10 litres	20 x 0.5 = 10 litres	10 x 1 = 10 litres
Air not reaching lungs	50 x 0.15 = 7.5 litres	20 x 0.15 = 3 litres	10 x 0.15 = 1.5 litres
Air reaching lungs	10 – 7.5 = 2.5 litres	10 – 3 = 7 litres	10 – 1.5 = 8.5 litres

BLOOD SUPPLY TO THE LUNGS

Each lung needs a good supply of blood, to allow collection of oxygen and elimination of carbon dioxide. This is provided by major blood vessels carrying blood directly to the lungs from the heart.

The circulation of blood from the heart to the lungs and back to the heart is a separate loop from the rest of the body. It is called the **pulmonary** circulation. In this loop, the heart pumps **deoxygenated** blood to the lungs and **oxygenated** blood flows back to the heart. In addition, the tissues of the lungs themselves are supplied with oxygenated blood by the bronchial arteries and deoxygenated blood is removed via the bronchial veins. This is part of the main circulatory loop of the body.

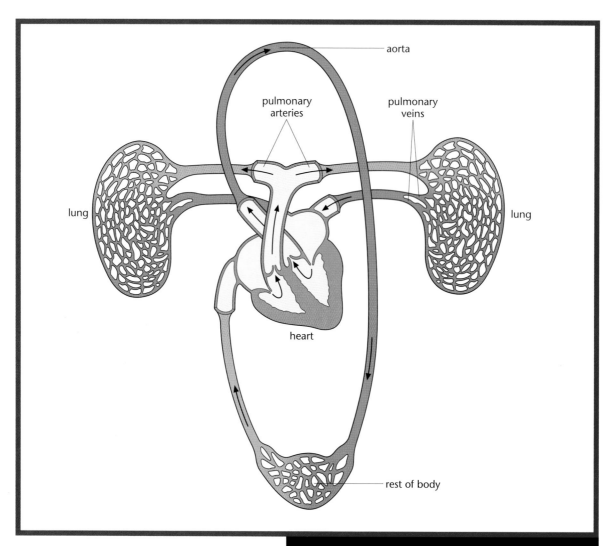

This diagram shows how the lungs are linked to the heart and major blood vessels.

Pulmonary circulation

Deoxygenated blood leaves the right side of the heart via the pulmonary trunk. This is very short, branching almost immediately into two – the right pulmonary artery, taking blood to the right lung, and the left pulmonary artery, taking blood to the left lung. The pulmonary arteries are the only arteries in the body that carry deoxygenated blood.

This photograph shows the capillaries, surrounding the alveoli, inside the lungs.

Inside each lung, the pulmonary arteries branch into smaller vessels, carrying blood to each lobe. These vessels branch again and again, eventually forming the very narrowest vessels, the **capillaries**. These have very thin walls to allow gases and other substances to move between the blood and body tissues by a process known as diffusion. This means that **molecules** of a particular gas or chemical move from a place where the concentration is high, to a place where the concentration is lower – balancing the concentration. As blood passes through the capillaries, it loses carbon dioxide and collects oxygen. Capillaries unite to form larger vessels and these rejoin to form the right pulmonary vein in the right lung, and the left pulmonary vein in the left lung. These large vessels carry freshly oxygenated blood back to the left side of the heart, from where it is pumped around to the rest of the body.

This complete circulation, from heart to lungs and back to the heart takes 4–8 seconds.

Blockage

A blockage in any part of the pulmonary circulation can be very serious. A blood clot, air bubble or a piece of debris can be carried around the body in large blood vessels, eventually reaching the heart. If something like this is pumped out of the heart and into the pulmonary circulation, it can become lodged in one of the smaller vessels inside the lungs and block the blood flow through the lung. This blockage is called a pulmonary embolism. A serious blockage can cause a patient to collapse in need of vital emergency treatment. However, even with good medical care, the patient may still die.

Most pulmonary embolisms are caused by blood clots, and are treated by drugs to make the clot dissolve. Other drugs, such as aspirin, can make the blood less sticky, reducing the risk of more clots forming in the future.

CHEST INVESTIGATIONS

The lungs are vital organs and it is important that they are working properly. Doctors can examine the lungs using a variety of techniques to determine what problems may be present and to decide on the best course of treatment.

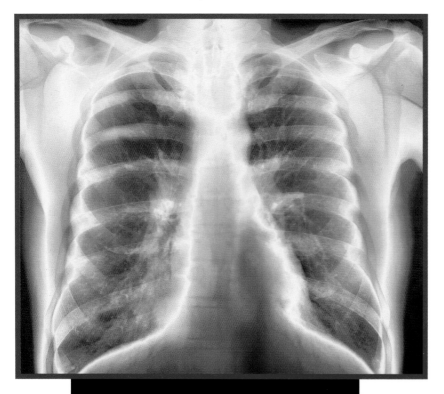

Chest X-ray

An X-ray gives information about the lung tissue. Diseased lung tissue blocks the path of X-rays more than healthy lung tissue does and so it shows up as a shadow (a white patch) on the X-ray. Shadows are usually seen as the result of infections, such as tuberculosis, or other diseases, such as lung cancer. Fluid build-up can also be detected by X-rays, indicating a possible disease such as pleurisy.

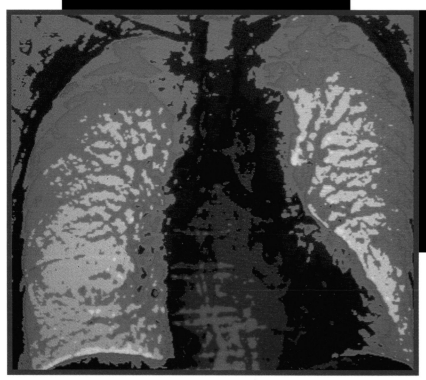

Mobile chest X-ray units can visit different places for detection of lung diseases.

The first picture (top left) shows a chest X-ray. The second picture (left) is a CAT scan, showing a lot more detailed information than that provided by the X-ray.

CAT scan

If doctors need more detailed information than an ordinary X-ray can provide, a CAT (computerized axial tomography) scan can be used. This shows the blood vessels and the airways inside the lungs, in a series of 'slices' through the chest. This allows doctors to pinpoint the precise location and extent of a disease. A CAT scan is about 100 times more sensitive than an ordinary X-ray.

For a CAT scan, patients lie still inside the scanner, which is like a large metal tube. The scan takes about 20 minutes, as the scanner is rotated a full 360° around the patient's body.

The scanner passes an X-ray beam through the body. This is picked up by a detector and the information is fed into a computer for analysis. An image is shown on a monitor with the most dense material showing up as white, less dense material as shades of grey and liquid and air as black. For extra clarity, colours may be used instead of just grey shades.

Bronchoscopy

During a bronchoscopy a flexible tube, containing hundreds of glass fibres, is inserted into the patient's trachea via the nose. When light shines on the glass fibres, they act like a tubular mirror and reflect the image back up to the eyepiece. This gives the doctor a clear picture of the inside surfaces of the airways. The bronchoscope can be manoeuvred around the main **bronchi**, and can be used to take samples. It is only useful for examination of the bigger airways, as it is too large to enter the narrower passages.

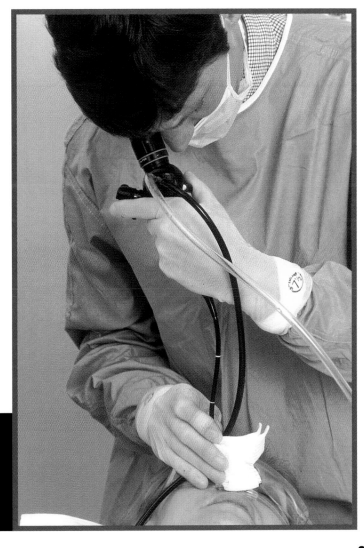

This asthma patient is being examined using a bronchoscope. The doctor will be able to take samples from her airways to examine under a microscope.

Pleurisy

Pleurisy is an infection of the **pleural membranes**, usually caused by **micro-organisms** that may enter the body via the airways during normal breathing. As the patient breathes in and out, the pleural membranes rub against each other, rather than sliding smoothly as they do in a healthy lung. This rubbing makes a scratchy, grating sound and causes intense pain. Sometimes, watery liquid or pus builds up in the pleural cavity and can be seen on an X-ray.

Treatment is usually with **antibiotics**, to kill the micro-organisms responsible, and painkillers, to help keep the patient comfortable. If a large amount of fluid and pus collects, it may be necessary to remove it. A special, hollow needle is inserted through the chest wall into the pleural cavity allowing the fluid to drain away.

Pneumonia

Pneumonia is an acute inflammation of the narrowest airways of the lungs. Fluid builds up in these airways, preventing the lungs from functioning normally. In the USA, there are an estimated 4 million cases every year – most commonly among young children, elderly people and smokers.

Pneumonia is caused by micro-organism infection, usually by a **bacterium** called *Streptococcus pneumoniae,* but other micro-organisms can also be responsible, entering the lungs via the airways during normal breathing.

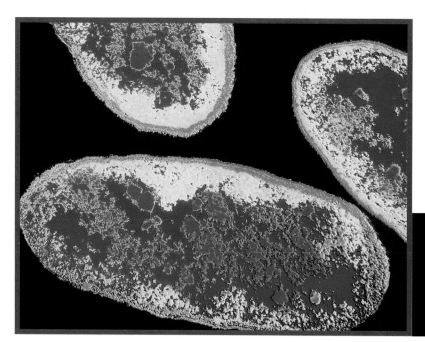

Pneumonia causes fever, chills, coughs, chest pains and tiredness. Patients are usually treated with antibiotics, to kill the micro-organisms, drugs, to clear the airways, and chest **physiotherapy**.

Aeromonas hydrophila is a bacteria associated with pneumonia that is resistant to many antibiotics, including penicillin.

Tuberculosis (TB)

Tuberculosis (TB) is caused by infection with the micro-organism *Mycobacterium tuberculosis.* The bacterium damages lung tissue, making holes in the lung that cannot be repaired. It can be passed on by contact with someone already infected, or by inhalation of the bacterium.

Worldwide, it is the most common infectious disease – there are an estimated 8 million new cases every year, with 3 million people dying from it annually. During the 20th century, tuberculosis has become much less common in developed countries, as housing conditions and diet have improved. Vaccination programmes in many countries have also helped to reduce the incidence of the disease, but in many poorer countries tuberculosis is still very common.

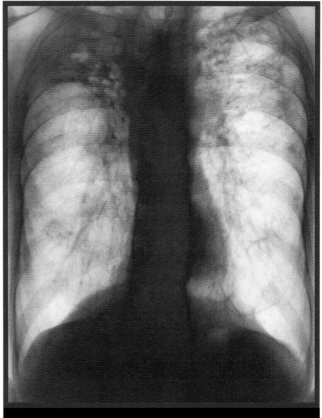

This is a chest X-ray of a person suffering from tuberculosis. The section coloured red in one of the lungs is the affected area.

Testing (Heaf or Mantoux tests) can show whether a person is immune to TB. A tiny amount of dead TB material is injected into the forearm, and the skin is examined again some days later. The dead TB material will not cause the patient to develop TB, but if the skin becomes red and swollen, it indicates that the person's immune system is responding to the TB material, and they are immune to the disease. If there is no reaction, the person has no immunity to the disease. Vaccination, usually with BCG (Bacille Calmette-Guérin, named after the doctors who introduced it) injects a dose of live, but harmless, mycobacterium, the micro-organism that causes tuberculosis. This stimulates the immune system, generating a long-lived immunity to TB.

Cystic fibrosis

Cystic fibrosis is an inherited disease that affects the lungs and other organs. Thick **mucus** is produced by the lungs and does not drain away easily. As it builds up, the airways become blocked and inflamed and the patient finds it difficult to breathe. Chest physiotherapy is needed every day to prevent mucus build-up, and antibiotics can help to reduce chest infections.

INSIDE THE LUNGS

The terminal **bronchioles** branch again to form tiny tubes called alveolar ducts. These lead into microscopic hollow balls called **alveoli** (one is an alveolus). The whole structure looks rather like a bunch of grapes, with the bronchioles as the stalk and the alveoli as the grapes.

Each lung contains more than 300 million alveoli. Although each is tiny, together they provide a huge internal surface area, many times greater than the surface area of the skin. A single alveolus is only about 0.025 millimetres in diameter – it would take about 40 to make one millimetre. The alveoli walls are thicker in some places than others, varying from less than 0.001 millimetres to 0.01 millimetres. At their thinnest, they are just a single cell thick, to allow gases – oxygen and carbon dioxide – to move between the alveoli and the blood capillaries. Each alveolus is closely surrounded by blood **capillaries** that form a network over its surface.

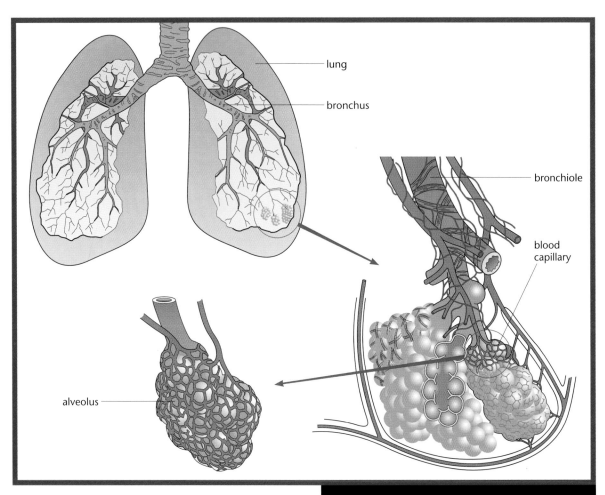

This series of pictures shows the structure of an area of lung, with increasing magnification.

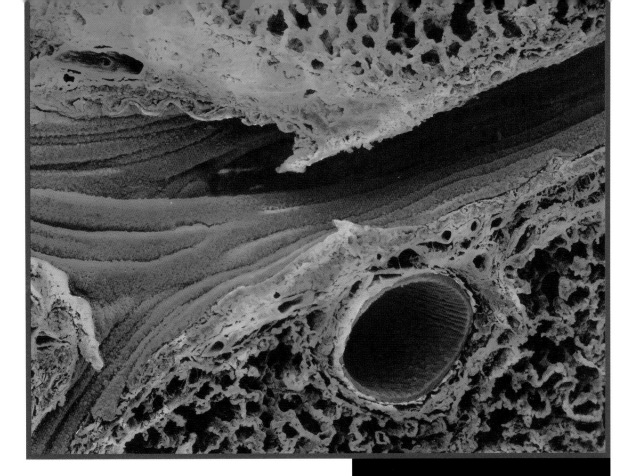

Alveolar fluid

The lining of each alveolus produces alveolar fluid, to keep the internal walls of the alveoli moist and to moisten the incoming air. Alveolar fluid also contains a substance called lung surfactant, which helps to keep the alveoli fully inflated. Lung surfactant works by reducing the surface tension of the water on the inner walls of the alveoli, preventing them collapsing inwards and sticking together.

In this coloured photomicrograph of lung tissue, we can see a cross-section of a pulmonary blood vessel (lower right, blue). The lung tissue (green) is made up of alveoli.

Babies do not breathe before birth, so their alveoli are not inflated and they do not need alveolar fluid. However, they need to breathe as soon as they are born, so the alveoli have to inflate. If there is not enough alveolar fluid, the alveoli may not inflate, or may inflate and collapse again so the baby is unable to breathe properly. Premature babies are particularly at risk from this and may need to spend some time in an incubator before they can breathe without assistance.

Alveolar walls

The alveolar walls do not have **cilia** to keep them free from debris. Instead, the alveoli contain specialized white blood cells. Some stick to the inside of the alveolar wall, and some move around freely inside the alveoli. They engulf and destroy **micro-organisms** and other foreign particles that enter the alveoli.

GASEOUS EXCHANGE

Breathing in and out is the mechanism by which the body gets rid of waste carbon dioxide and collects fresh oxygen. This swapping of one gas for another takes place in the **alveoli**. The process is called gaseous exchange, and it occurs by diffusion. This means that **molecules** of a gas move from an area of high concentration to one where the concentration is lower – balancing the concentration.

Gaseous exchange is possible only because the walls of the blood **capillaries** and the walls of the alveoli are very close to each other, and are so thin that gas molecules can pass through them in both directions.

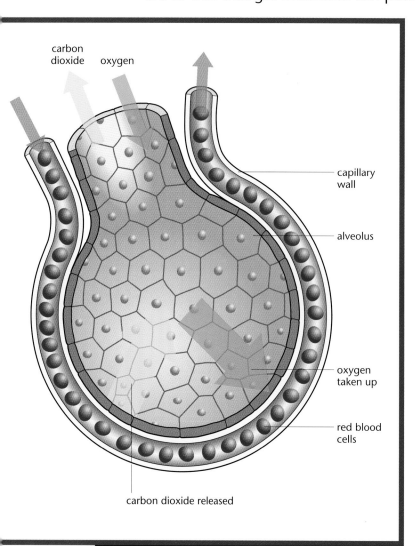

carbon dioxide

oxygen

capillary wall

alveolus

oxygen taken up

red blood cells

carbon dioxide released

This diagram shows how gases are exchanged as blood passes through the capillaries in the lungs. Oxygen diffuses out of the alveolus into the blood. Carbon dioxide diffuses in the opposite direction.

When we breathe in, the alveoli fill with air, which has a high concentration of oxygen. The blood in the capillaries has a low oxygen concentration. This means that the oxygen levels are unbalanced, and the oxygen in the alveoli moves to even this out. Oxygen molecules spread out and dissolve in the thin layer of fluid that lines the inside of the alveolar walls. They can then move through the alveolar wall, through the capillary wall and into the blood, where they get picked up by the red blood cells.

At the same time, the blood flowing through the capillaries is rich in carbon dioxide. A tiny amount is carried by red blood cells, but most of it is dissolved in the plasma, the liquid part of the blood. The air in the alveoli contains less carbon dioxide, so the carbon dioxide molecules move out of the blood, through the capillary wall, through the alveolar wall and into the alveoli. It then leaves the alveoli as we breathe out.

Blood capillaries are just large enough for red blood cells to squeeze through, as this photomicrograph shows.

Diffusion

This movement of molecules from a place where the concentration is high to a place where the concentration is low is called diffusion. It happens all the time in the air around us.

If you spray some perfume at one end of a room, the smell will eventually reach a person at the other end of the room. This happens because the perfume molecules move through the air from the place where there is a high concentration (next to the perfume bottle), to the place where there is little (further across the room). This movement of the molecules continues until they are spread evenly throughout the room.

Oxygen is carried around in the red blood cells by a large molecule called **haemoglobin**. Oxygen joins on to the haemoglobin and can be detached when it is needed elsewhere in the body.

Carbon monoxide poisoning

Another gas, carbon monoxide, can also join on to haemoglobin. It prevents oxygen joining on to haemoglobin, so if carbon monoxide is inhaled – less oxygen can be carried around the body. Eventually the body cells become so starved of oxygen that the person dies. This is known as carbon monoxide poisoning. Some household appliances, such as old gas fires, can emit carbon monoxide – so it makes sense to install special detectors that alert you if there is too much carbon monoxide in a room.

Car exhausts contain carbon monoxide, too so it is not a good idea to sit in a car with the engine running in a confined space such as a garage.

Carbon monoxide also competes with oxygen for haemoglobin in people who smoke cigarettes. One fifth of a smoker's haemoglobin may be bound to carbon monoxide and therefore be unable to transport oxygen around the body.

ASTHMA

Asthma is becoming increasingly common. Doctors think this may be due to a variety of changes in our diets and in our environment. It causes coughing, wheezing and breathlessness, but can usually be controlled with medication. There are several different types of asthma, but in most young people asthma is caused by an **allergy** to something in the environment.

Causes of asthma

The most common cause of asthma in children and teenagers is an allergy to something in their environment, such as pollen, house dust, pet fur or air pollution. In patients who develop asthma when they are older, there are probably other triggers, such as medicines or chemicals with which they work. Asthma attacks can also be triggered by exercise, breathing in cold air or emotional upsets.

Allergy tests can be carried out to find if there is a specific trigger – something **inhaled**, eaten or touched – that leads to an asthma attack. In many cases, once the person knows what causes their asthma they are able to avoid it completely or at least keep their exposure to it to a minimum.

Symptoms

In patients suffering from asthma, the **bronchi** are inflamed. They swell, so they become narrower, restricting the flow of air into and out of the lungs. When muscles in the walls of the airways are irritated, they contract, making the airways even narrower and making breathing more difficult. The inflammation also means that too much sticky **mucus** is produced, which blocks the airways even more.

Treatment

Asthma can be treated with drugs. Many patients have inhalers, which they can use to deliver the drugs when they need them. There are two types of inhaler:
- reliever inhalers can be used to help relieve a specific attack; they are used only when needed
- preventer inhalers are used to control the underlying inflammation; they need to be taken regularly, even when the patient has no symptoms, to prevent further attacks.

Patients may have either or both of these types of inhaler, depending on the problems they have. As with all medicines, it is important that you only take what has been prescribed for you personally – somebody else's inhaler may look identical to yours, but it could contain a very different medicine.

Asthma and sport

Many people with asthma play sports regularly. This is fine, but it is very important that they carry their inhalers with them at all times. Exercise can sometimes trigger an attack, and it is no good having an inhaler in your sports bag if that is in the changing room at one end of the pitch while you are having an asthma attack at the other end! It is also important to let somebody else (like a teacher) know you are asthmatic so that if there are any problems they can tell a doctor or paramedic.

Asthma attacks

Severe asthma attacks can require emergency treatment. Bronchodilator drugs need to be given immediately. They relieve the spasm and widen the airways so that the patient can breathe normally again. The most effective way of delivering these drugs is via a nebuliser; this produces a fine mist of the drug dissolved in water, which the patient inhales through a mask or mouthpiece. After a severe attack, a patient may need to take some **steroid** drugs for a while to reduce the inflammation and the risk of another attack.

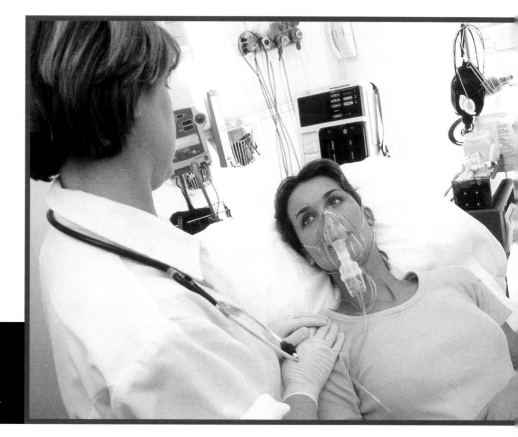

This patient has been given an oxygen mask to help her to breathe.

LUNGS AND AIR POLLUTION

There are many sources and types of air pollution; some are found generally in the air around us and others are found in restricted areas. Air pollution can cause a variety of breathing difficulties and lung problems. Governments, companies and individual people are trying to find ways of reducing air pollution and exposure to it.

Air pollution levels can be very different in different places, and even in one place at different times. It is often thought of as a modern problem, but has been around ever since people began to build factories with smoking chimneys. In the late 19th century, an environmental officer in northern England noted that the smoke from chimneys was black with soot particles and so acidic that it was eating away metal and stone. The use of smokeless fuels in some places, and also stricter laws have helped to reduce this kind of problem. However, in other ways air pollution has become significantly worse in recent years as the use of motor vehicles has increased.

Air pollution can trigger many lung problems; weather forecasts often contain data about expected pollution levels so that people who are vulnerable, such as the elderly and those who suffer from asthma, can protect themselves accordingly.

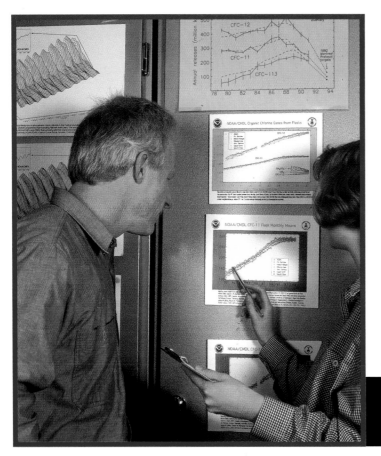

Measures to reduce pollution

As we begin to realize the amount of damage air pollution can do to our health and to the environment, measures are being introduced to reduce it. Cars with catalytic converters break down the harmful carbon monoxide and nitrogen oxide of exhaust fumes to harmless gases, but do still produce some pollutants. Lead-free and low-sulfur petrol also reduce the pollution. Many industrial chimneys are now fitted with special filters to clean the gases

Scientists collect statistical information to measure air pollution levels.

before they are released into the atmosphere. We have done a lot – but most people would agree that there is still a lot more to do.

Pneumoconiosis

Pneumoconiosis is a group of diseases resulting from the air pollution that some people are exposed to because of the jobs they do. They are all caused by **inhalation** of different types of dust particles over a long period of time, resulting in inflammation and damage to the lungs. Healthy tissue is replaced by scar tissue and in some cases pneumoconiosis may lead to lung cancer.

In developed countries, people working in conditions where they may be exposed to potentially harmful air pollutants are required to wear protective clothing such as face masks. If the risk is high, such as in demolishing buildings that contain asbestos, breathing apparatus may be needed. In poorer countries, however, such precautions are often not available.

In busy cities, some people try to avoid inhaling polluted air by wearing masks that filter out the pollutants.

Treatment

Treatment of these diseases depends on the extent and seriousness of the lung damage caused. In some cases, drugs and oxygen therapy may help to relieve the symptoms. In others, surgery to remove damaged lung tissue may be appropriate.

Disease	Cause	People affected
asbestosis	asbestos fibres	builders and demolition workers
silicosis	silicon particles	silicon miners
anthracosis	coal dust	coal miners
fibrosing alveolitis or 'Farmer's lung'	hay, straw, other farm materials	farmers and others associated with livestock

SMOKING

Cigarette smoke causes serious damage to the lungs and other parts of the body. This can lead to diseases that, in many cases, are fatal. The contents of cigarette smoke are addictive, making it difficult to give it up – so it really does make sense not to start in the first place!

The components of cigarette smoke

The lungs of a healthy person are pale and clean. The tar and smoke from cigarettes collects in the lungs of a smoker, making them dirty and blocking the tiny **alveoli**. This leads to a general decrease in the ability of the lungs to work efficiently. Cigarette smoke has three main components: tar, carbon monoxide and nicotine. Each damages the body in some way:

- *tar*: this irritates the lining of the airways, destroying the **cilia** that usually sweep out dust and **micro-organisms**. **Mucus** builds up, leading to infection and inflammation, and a 'smoker's cough' develops as the person repeatedly tries to clear the airways. Eventually, bronchitis and emphysema may develop.
- *carbon monoxide*: this affects the arteries, causing them to harden and narrow. The heart has to work harder to pump blood around the body, so all activities and exercise take more effort and even small movements can cause breathlessness.
- *nicotine*: this is a drug, and it is the part of the smoke to which people become addicted. Many smokers say that it helps them to stay calm and relaxed – but it also leads to high blood pressure, clogged blood vessels and heart disease.

Scientists have shown that the combined effects of the components of cigarette smoke can lead to serious illnesses, such as cancer of the mouth, throat and lungs, heart disease, stroke, chronic bronchitis and emphysema.

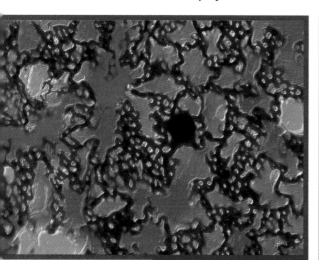
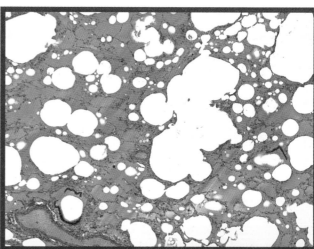

The picture on the left shows a section from a normal lung. The picture on the right shows a section from a lung that has been damaged by emphysema. The white areas are the enlarged and damaged aveoli.

Women smokers

Pregnant women who smoke put their babies at risk. Doctors have found that babies born to mothers who smoked while pregnant are smaller, lighter and weaker than babies of non-smokers. Babies of smoking mothers have also been shown to have an increased risk of heart and breathing problems.

Smoking can have other unpleasant side effects too, including:
- wrinkles around eyes and mouth, speeding up ageing of the skin
- yellowed hair and fingers
- brown, stained teeth
- bad breath
- varicose veins.

Passive smoking

Passive smoking is another serious problem. If a person in a room is smoking, the cigarette smoke does not just stay close to them – it drifts around the room, mixing with the rest of the air. Anybody else in the room will have to breathe in the cigarette smoke, too. This can lead to illness, and potentially the death of the non-smoker. Smoking is now banned in many public places, such as offices, shops, hospitals and some trains. In many companies workers are only permitted to smoke outside the building.

If cigarette smoke collects in a room, as in this picture, even the non-smokers have to inhale it. If parents continue to smoke around their children they are putting them at risk.

Giving up smoking

Smoking is linked to some dangerous diseases. Scientists and doctors generally agree that smokers are not likely to live as long as non-smokers are; they are also more likely to be disabled by smoking-related diseases. To make people aware of the damage they may be doing to themselves by smoking, many countries now have laws making every cigarette packet carry a health warning.

There are a variety of things available to help people to stop smoking, such as nicotine gum, nicotine patches and dummy cigarettes. Doctors can also prescribe some drugs for people who need extra help to give up smoking.

Lungs cannot draw air into themselves – they need to be blown up and then deflated, rather like blowing air into a balloon and then letting the air rush out of it. **Inhaling** and **exhaling** requires the co-ordination of contraction and relaxation of the **diaphragm** and muscles in the ribcage and abdomen.

Inhalation

Inhalation is an active event – muscles have to contract to make it happen:

- diaphragm contracts: this makes the diaphragm flatter, and it moves downwards away from the chest space
- **intercostal** muscles between the ribs contract: this moves the ribcage and **sternum** upwards and outwards.

These two actions make the chest space larger, so the air pressure (the force of air pushing on the airways) inside the chest is lower than the air pressure outside. Air is drawn into the lungs until the pressure inside equals that outside.

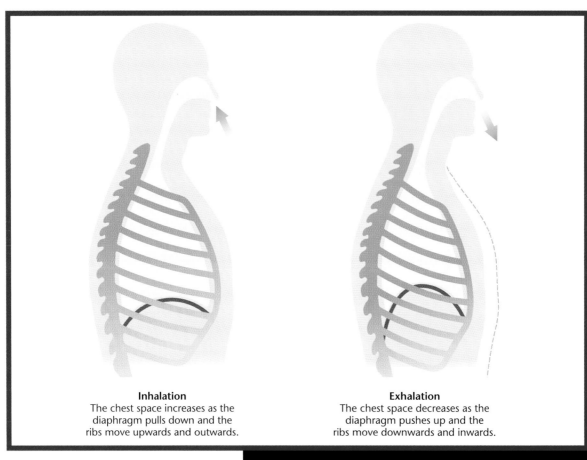

Inhalation
The chest space increases as the diaphragm pulls down and the ribs move upwards and outwards.

Exhalation
The chest space decreases as the diaphragm pushes up and the ribs move downwards and inwards.

These diagrams show how the movements of the ribs and diaphragm are important in breathing.

Exhalation

Exhalation is a passive event – it happens naturally as muscles relax back to their resting positions, like an elastic band springing back after it has been stretched:

- diaphragm relaxes: it becomes more dome-shaped, and pushes upwards towards the chest space
- intercostal muscles relax: this allows the ribs and sternum to move downwards and inwards.

These muscle relaxations make the chest space smaller, so the air pressure inside the chest is higher than the air pressure outside. Air is forced out of the chest, until the pressures inside and outside are equal.

Lying down

Have you ever wondered why patients in hospitals are propped up on their pillows?

If you lie flat on your back, gravity pulls the abdominal organs down so that they push against the diaphragm. This makes it harder for the diaphragm to contract, so inhalation is difficult. Although we usually sleep lying flat, our respiratory systems would function more easily if we propped ourselves up a little. Raising the head and shoulders into a half-sitting position means that gravity pulls the abdominal organs down, away from the diaphragm, and also pulls on the diaphragm itself, so inhalation becomes easier.

BREATHING CONTROL

We can control our breathing for a short while but usually, whether we are awake or asleep, active or resting, we breathe without thinking about it. Breathing is controlled by involuntary signals from the brain, but these in turn are regulated by feedback from the rest of the body. The respiratory centre in the brain controls the contraction of the muscles involved in breathing. It is situated in the **brain stem**, in areas called the medulla oblongata and the pons.

With training and practise, people can exert a lot of control over their breathing, which is needed in order to play instruments such as a trumpet.

In normal, resting breathing **inhalation** lasts for just under 2 seconds, and **exhalation** for just under 3 seconds. The respiratory centre has two separate circuits of nerve cells that work alternately. One circuit, the I circuit, triggers inhalation and the other, the E circuit, triggers exhalation.

Fast and slow

Sometimes, we need to breathe more quickly or more slowly, so it is important that the respiratory centre responds to what is happening in the rest of the body:

- *carbon dioxide concentration*: if the level of carbon dioxide in the blood begins to increase, the respiratory centre will speed up the breathing rate
- *exercise*: when we exercise, signals from sensors in joints and muscles are relayed to the respiratory centre, and the breathing rate is increased
- *lungs*: stretch receptors in the lungs send signals to the respiratory centre, giving information about how much the lungs are stretched.

We can consciously stop or change our breathing pattern for a short time, as the cerebral cortex (the part of the brain that deals with our thoughts) can override the respiratory centre. However, as soon as the carbon dioxide levels in the blood begin to rise, the respiratory centre takes control again and normal breathing resumes, whether we want it to or not!

Swimming and diving

Control of breathing is very important for swimmers and divers. Swimmers need to match their breathing with their strokes. For example, in breaststroke, the head lifts as the hands push backwards, making it easy to take a breath; but as the hands push forwards the head dips underwater, making it impossible to take a breath. Divers need to take a large breath in before they hit the water, so that they have enough air to last until they surface and can breathe again.

For most people, for most of the time, there is plenty of air around us for normal breathing. However, some people go into situations where there is little or no air and so they need to have their own air supply with them.

Underwater divers

Swimming just below the surface of the water is possible using a snorkel – a short hollow pipe allows you to breathe without having to come to the surface. To dive deeper, an air supply is needed. Divers who are not going to great depths carry tanks of compressed air (air at a higher pressure than in the atmosphere) strapped to their backs, connected to a mouthpiece by a hose. For diving to greater depths, other mixtures of gases may be used. Nitrox is a mixture of nitrogen and oxygen, with more oxygen and less nitrogen than normal air. Some divers use a mixture of helium and oxygen without any nitrogen, and others use a mixture of all three gases.

Decompression sickness

The deeper a diver goes, the greater the pressure of the water on his or her body. As the pressure increases, so does the amount of nitrogen that can dissolve in the liquid of the blood. This does not cause a problem, until the diver wants to return to the surface. If the diver

Humans cannot breathe underwater, so divers need to take their own air supply.

comes up too quickly, the pressure decreases too quickly and the nitrogen dissolved in the blood comes out of solution as bubbles of gas. The bubbles are carried around the body in the blood and may lodge in the joints, causing a lot of pain. This is called decompression sickness, or 'the bends' and it can be fatal. Divers avoid it by coming up very slowly so that the nitrogen diffuses out of the blood without forming bubbles.

Firefighters

Firefighters need breathing apparatus to allow them to enter smoke-filled buildings. There is plenty of air in the buildings, but the smoke mixed with the air would choke them very quickly. In industrial fires and explosions, dangerous chemicals may be released into the air and so firefighters need breathing apparatus to supply breathable air. Cylinders of compressed air are strapped to their backs. Modern breathing devices have inbuilt communications systems and personal alarms.

Astronauts

There is no atmosphere in space, so astronauts must have their own oxygen supply if they are to leave the safe environment of a space centre or shuttle. They use a PLSS – Primary Life Support System with a backpack that supplies oxygen, maintains the air pressure and temperature, and absorbs moisture and carbon dioxide. Their spacesuits are maintained at a lower pressure than that inside the space shuttle, so they have the opposite problem to deep sea divers – if they go straight out, they will suffer from decompression sickness as nitrogen bubbles out of their blood. They have to spend several hours breathing pure oxygen before they step out into space. This removes any nitrogen that is dissolved in their body fluids and prevents bubbles forming when the pressure is suddenly reduced. NASA is developing new spacesuits that will maintain a higher pressure, to reduce this problem.

The effects of altitude

As you climb higher and higher, the amount of oxygen in the atmosphere decreases. People from lower areas who visit areas of high altitude may suffer from altitude sickness; the lack of oxygen makes them feel tired, dizzy, faint and sick. People who live in high altitudes all the time are able to breathe normally because their bodies have adapted to the lack of oxygen by producing extra red blood cells. This also means that athletes from those areas are able to achieve outstanding performances at lower altitudes. Mountaineers who attempt to climb very high peaks avoid altitude sickness by climbing to one level and then resting for a few days, giving their bodies time to get used to the lack of oxygen before climbing even higher.

BREATHING EMERGENCIES

We need to breathe to stay alive, so anything that interrupts the breathing process is potentially very serious. Some can be dealt with easily, while others may require specialized treatment.

Choking

It is quite common to choke on a piece of food and usually this can be dislodged by coughing. If that does not work, a trained first-aider can use the 'Heimlich Manoeuvre' to force the food out. Unless this procedure is carried out properly, the liver, ribs and lungs may be damaged – so leave it to the experts!

Anaphylactic shock

Anaphylactic shock is the result of an **allergic reaction**. Most allergies simply cause a rash or an itch, but sometimes when a person is exposed to something to which they are allergic – such as peanuts or a wasp sting – their body may react very swiftly. The airways get narrower, restricting the flow of air and causing wheeziness. It must be treated quickly, with an injection of epinephrine to reverse the effects and open the airways. People likely to suffer from this often wear a **medi-bracelet** and carry their epinephrine in an **epi-pen**.

Suffocation

A person suffocates if they do not get enough oxygen. This can be as a result of:

- *strangulation* – something tied around the throat preventing the flow of air into and out of the lungs
- *drowning* – a muscle spasm in the throat prevents too much water entering the lungs, but it also prevents airflow
- *choking* – a foreign object blocks the airways
- *blockage* – nose and mouth blocked preventing air entering airways
- *gases* – breathing in carbon monoxide stops the blood transporting oxygen.

All of these prevent air getting to the lungs, so the body becomes starved of oxygen. Our brains cannot work without oxygen so death follows within minutes.

First aid

Knowing how to help someone who is in difficulty can be very useful. Why not find out more about first aid – you could get a book from a library, look on the Internet or join an organization, such as the Red Cross or St. John's Ambulance Brigade?

Artificial resuscitation – the kiss of life

If a person has stopped breathing, it is important to get oxygen into their body. Although the air we **exhale** contains less oxygen than the air around us, there is still enough oxygen in it to keep a person alive. The main steps of artificial resuscitation are:

- clear the airway of any blockage
- tip the person's head back to open their airways
- hold the nose closed
- seal your lips over the person's lips
- blow exhaled air into the person's lungs
- check that their chest rises
- move your mouth away to let air escape from the person's lungs
- take another breath and repeat.

If a person's heart has stopped beating too, **CPR (cardio-pulmonary resuscitation)** may be needed. These methods are simple, but can save lives – and many organizations, such as the St. John's Ambulance Brigade train ordinary people in how to carry them out.

These medical students are using special dummies to practise giving the kiss of life to patients.

WHAT CAN GO WRONG WITH MY LUNGS?

This book has explained the different parts of the lungs and airways, why they are important and how they can be damaged by injury and illness. This page summarizes some of the problems that can affect young people. It also gives you information about how each problem is treated.

Many problems can also be avoided by good health behaviour. This is called prevention. Taking regular exercise and getting plenty of rest are important, as is eating a balanced diet. This is important in your teenage years, when your body is still developing. The table tells you some of the ways you can prevent injury and illness.

Remember, if you think something is wrong with your body, you should always talk to a trained medical professional, like a doctor or a school nurse. Regular medical check-ups are an important part of maintaining a healthy body.

Illness or injury	Cause	Symptoms	Prevention	Treatment
Asthma	Swelling and narrowing of **bronchi**, often due to an **allergic reaction**, cold air, exercise or an emotional upset.	Coughing, wheezing, breathlessness – all making breathing difficult.	Identification and avoidance of whatever triggers an allergic reaction.	Drugs delivered via inhalers: a reliever for treating a specific attack and a preventer used regularly to prevent attacks.
Laryngitis	Infection by **virus** or **bacteria**, violent shouting, irritation by cigarette smoke.	Sore throat, difficulty speaking, hoarse voice or inability to make any sound.	Avoid shouting too loudly. Avoid cigarette smoke.	Rest voice completely for a few days. **Inhaling** warm steam can help, too.

Illness or injury	Cause	Symptoms	Prevention	Treatment
Tonsillitis	Infection, usually by bacteria.	Sore throat and difficulty swallowing; there may be earache and a stiff neck, too.	Maintain good general health with balanced diet. Maintain good oral hygiene.	Drink warm liquids and eat soft foods. Painkillers and **antibiotics** may be prescribed. Tonsils may be removed in severe cases.
Pleurisy	Usually infection of **pleural membranes** by **micro-organisms**.	Intense pain accompanied by scratchy, grating breathing.	Maintain good general health with balanced diet and regular exercise.	Antibiotics and painkillers. In severe cases, it may be necessary to drain excess fluid out of the chest.
Pneumonia	Inflammation of the lungs usually caused by micro-organism infection.	Fever, chills, cough, chest pain, tiredness.	Maintain good general health with balanced diet and regular exercise.	Antibiotics and possibly chest **physiotherapy**.

Further reading

Horrible Science, Blood, Bones and Body Bits, Nick Arnold, Tony de Saulles (Scholastic Hippo, 1996)
The Human Machine, The Power Pack: All about your heart, lungs and circulation, Sarah Angliss, Graham Rosewarne (Illustrator) (Belitha Press, 1999)
Human Physiology and Health, David Wright (Heinemann Educational, 2000)
Look at Your Body, Lungs, Steve Parker (Franklin Watts, 1996)
Need to Know, Tobacco, Sean Connolly (Heinemann Library, 2000)

GLOSSARY

aerobic respiration process using oxygen to release energy from glucose

allergic reaction reaction by the body to an antigen to which it is sensitive, such as the runny nose and sore eyes (reaction) of hay fever sufferers when exposed to pollens (antigen)

allergy sensitivity to a particular antigen that may lead to an allergic reaction

alveoli tiny air sacs of the lung

anaerobic respiration process releasing energy from glucose without using oxygen

antibiotic drug used to destroy harmful bacteria and fungi

bacteria group of micro-organisms that can cause infections

brain stem part of the brain that relays messages between the brain and the spinal cord

bronchiole narrow airway formed by the branching of a bronchus

bronchus one of the two airways (bronchi) formed by the branching of the trachea

capillary very fine blood vessel that links arteries to veins

carbohydrate nutrient that is broken down to release energy

cartilage strong, flexible material that protects bones

chemical reaction change in which one or more substances are turned into different substances

cilia microscopic hairs on the surfaces of some airways

CPR (cardio-pulmonary resuscitation) method which may be used in an emergency to help a person who has stopped breathing

decongestant drug that may be taken to reduce the amount of mucus in the airways

deoxygenated without oxygen

diaphragm strong sheet of muscle that forms the bottom of the chest space

epi-pen small container with a sterile needle attached that allows immediate administration of adrenalin by injection into a muscle, usually the thigh

exhale breathe out

exothermic giving off heat

haemoglobin molecule in red blood cells to which oxygen binds

hormones chemicals that are produced by the body, and travel around the body to affect other parts

influenza viral infection, commonly called 'flu'

inhale breathe in

intercostal word meaning 'between the ribs'

lung capacity maximum amount of air that can be held in the lungs

medi-bracelet chain with an identity tag that gives information for para-medics about a person's allergy and what should be done if they begin to suffer an anaphylactic reaction

membrane thin, covering layer of tissue

micro-organsim tiny living thing that can only be seen under a microscope

molecule smallest unit or particle of a substance made of two or more joined atoms

mucus sticky, slimy fluid that provides lubrication inside many organs and vessels

nasal cavity space inside the skull at the top of the nose

oxygenated with oxygen

physiotherapy treatment of disease or injury by massage and movement

pleural membrane membrane surrounding the lungs

protein type of large molecule that makes up some of the basic structures of all living things

pulmonary to do with the lungs

sensory to do with the senses

sinus hollow spaces inside some cranial and facial bones

sternum breastbone

steroid class of drugs that may be used for a variety of reasons, including reduction of inflammation

tendon strong fibres that connect muscles to bones

vertebra one of the bones of the spine

virus very small micro-organism that can cause infection

INDEX